Torch Tips for a Luminous Life

James Lloyd

9 Screens International
Newbury Park, CA

Published by 9 Screens, International
39 Edgar Court
Newbury Park, CA 91320

Publisher's Cataloging-in-Publication Data
Lloyd, James.
        Torch tips for a luminous life / James Lloyd.
–Newbury Park, CA: 9 Screens International, 2006

ISBN - 10: 0-9728427-2-1
ISBN - 13: 9780972842723

Printed in the United States of America
09 08 07 06*3 2 1
Library of Congress Control Number: 2006928083

Cover design and graphics by Bo Criss Design
Edited by Tanya Wisotsky Lloyd

DEDICATION

"What happens when your soul
Begins to awake in this world

To our deep need to love
And serve the Friend?

O the Beloved
Will send you
One of His wonderful, wild companions —
Like Hafiz."

- Hafiz

In my case He sent me one of His
most wonderful, wild companions —
Tamara Keefe.

I think God realized that I could no
longer recognize Him (or Her)
through any organization.
So He sent one of His angels to remind
me that He is LOVE and I am loved.

Could a greater gift be given?

Thank you, God...

Thank you, Tamara...

- James

DEDICATION

"Making the decision to have a child –
it's momentous.
It is to decide forever to have your heart
go walking around outside your body."

- Elizabeth Stone

I have heard that parents should be authority figures rather than friends to their children. Hmmm... I guess I blew that one. Not only am I friends with my daughters – we are best friends.

As they have grown from girls into young ladies, my goal has been for them to stay close friends. I realize I will not always be around, so I pray they will continue to remain close. And I know they will. They have remarkably different personalities, but do share one delightful trait:

They both have pure hearts.

I have often expressed the following, with much sobriety and deep conviction:

"I would not hesitate to die for either of my daughters, and I would smile doing so."

Thank you, Alexandra.

Thank you, Natasha.

Affectionately,

Dad

CONTENTS

INTRODUCTION

How do you view your life today?

Is it a candle...or is it a torch?

Is it just flickering or is it burning brightly?

The following passionate quote from George Bernard Shaw sparked the flame that became this book:

*"I am of the opinion that my life belongs to the whole community...
as long as I live, it is my privilege to do for it whatever I can.
I want to be thoroughly used up when I die. For the harder I
work, the more I live. I rejoice in life, for its own sake. Life is no
brief candle to me; it is a splendid torch, which I've got hold of for
the moment. And I want to make it burn as brightly as possible,
before handing it on to future generations."*

Throughout my life, I've had the privilege of getting up on
stages all over the world and speaking to people, helping
them find motivation and inspiration in their professional
and personal lives. In the process, I have been blessed to
learn from so many of them. I've been honored to share
hopes, fears, strategies, laughter, and warmth with them,
my family, and close friends. And I've gained a little insight
– and a lot of joy – along the way.

I would never claim to be the world's expert on passion
or "luminous living." I am only a man who has noticed
countless, remarkable qualities in others, and then compiled
them for our benefit.

I do make an effort every day to make sure my torch is burning brightly. And in the same way that the Olympic flame gets passed on from one person to the next, I, too, am honored to hand to you some of the helpful tips I've discovered.

May these thoughts spark the flame within each of us, as we strive to live positive, luminous lives.

– James

The Arts

Torch Tip #1
Master the art of greeting others.

*"There are two types of people. Those who come
into a room and say, 'Well, here I am!' and
those who come in and say, 'Ah, there you are.'"*

– Frederick Collins

With a wince, I confess I chose the less noble option for
many years. As a minister, I allowed my ego to run rampant.
Of course I would have never uttered the words, "Well, here
I am." But, sadly, that was my attitude. Thankfully, I have
repented, and I now work hard to honor others.

It is my theory that the first moment of interaction says it
all. Think about it: in just one second, the person to whom
we are speaking is able to perceive how excited we are. What
tone of voice are we using? What about our body language?

I am especially challenged with this concept as I walk into
my home after a day at work, sometimes half expecting a
welcome home party. It is so easy to enter with an attitude
of, "Well, here I am." Thankfully, I have a friend whose
example I strive to emulate – my dog, Phoebe. She is a
beautiful golden longhair Chihuahua. Although she is
housebroken, Phoebe has a "tiny accident" while greeting
me every day at the front door. I don't scold her because
she can't help it. She is just so excited to see me, she loses
her control. What an example! What if we all greeted one
another the same way?

(Occasionally my analogies go a bit too far.)

"You can make more friends in two months by becoming interested in other people than you can in two years by trying to get other people interested in you."

– Dale Carnegie

– INVITATION –

The next time you greet someone, say with your words, your eyes, and your heart,

"Ah, there you are!"

Torch Tip #2
Master the art of listening.

"When people talk, listen completely. Most people never listen."

– Ernest Hemingway

I once attended a workshop in San Diego to study the art and practice of dialogue but, ironically, it was mostly about listening. You can imagine how hard it was to spend three days in a room with 25 people and just listen to them! I thought, "I'm a professional speaker – this is difficult to sit here and only listen." But the stillness that happens when you're really listening opens up space for so many positive things to happen.

Sue, our workshop leader, gave us some homework: "Tonight, call a person you sometimes have difficulty listening to, and just listen. Listen completely, for as long as the person wants. Don't interrupt, don't end the call early, just listen."

I considered the fact that one of my favorite quotes is "I don't like people to talk while I'm interrupting." I knew this assignment was definitely going to be an interesting challenge for me.

It didn't take long to remember who was most often cut off in conversations when I had "heard enough," even though she may have felt she wasn't finished. So, I called my wife Tanya. It was 7:00 at night, and I figured that this phone call would be no longer than 15 minutes...I'd still have time to watch that ball game. Well, I tell you, 7:15 and 7:30 came and went. My wife was talking, and I was actively listening:

"Tell me more, Tanya."
"How did that make you feel?"
"Oh, that must have been frustrating!"

And it continued.

Two hours later, as the ball game ended, I realized that this was one of the longest phone calls I'd ever had! Finally, Tanya said, "Honey, I've really enjoyed our conversation. Thanks for listening. By the way, was this your homework assignment?"

I started laughing and told her how much I had learned in the workshop – and during our conversation. From that moment on, I resolved to be a better listener.

In his phenomenally popular book *The Power of Now*, Eckhart Tolle writes: "When listening to another person, don't just listen with your mind, listen with your whole body. You are giving the other person space – space to be. It is the most precious gift you can give."

> *"There is a difference between listening*
> *and waiting for your turn to speak."*
>
> *– Lisa Ford*

– I N V I T A T I O N –

Listen intently today,
and allow others to finish conversations.

Torch Tip #3
Master the art of apologizing.

*"In America today, we have mastered the art
of almost apologizing."*

– James Lloyd

Most of us know that insincere, halfhearted apologies are
worthless! Listen in on a conversation I often had with my
daughters when they were younger:

"What do you say to your sister?"
"Sorry!"
"And what do you say?"
"Sorry!"

Can you hear the insincerity?

In our generation, we have mastered the art of almost
apologizing:

"Well, I'm sorry *if* I hurt your feelings."
Instead, how about "I'm sorry I hurt your feelings"?

"I'm sorry, *but* you had *no* right..."
Instead, how about "I am sorry I said that"?
Saying "but" destroys the apology.

As Martha Beck writes in the September 2004 issue of
O, the Oprah Magazine: "A lame, badly-constructed apology
can do more damage than the original offense... Apologizing
is rarely comfortable or easy, so if you're going to do it at all,
make it count."

Most importantly – *apologies must be specific*...so give the
reason for the apology.

Recently I saw a newspaper article about a woman who said she had an apology disorder – now it's some kind of medical disorder that keeps us from apologizing?! Well, if I have any kind of apology disorder, it most certainly involves my ego. I know that in order to say "I'm sorry," I need to put down my ego and pick up my courage and humility. Doing this will yield untold benefits.

Remember when the baseball commissioner told the banished Pete Rose that if he just apologized for betting on baseball, he'd probably get reinstated into baseball? For Pete's sake, apologize!

"An apology is a good way to have the last word."

– Author unknown

– I N V I T A T I O N –

Does someone deserve an apology from you right now?
If so, put this book down and go apologize
– fully and sincerely.

Master the art of forgiving.

"The weak can never forgive.
Forgiveness is the attribute of the strong."

– Mahatma Gandhi

Forgiveness. It's tough, and it's complicated.

On one of my business trips, I had the pleasure of hearing a speech by Jackie Pflug. Jackie was a flight attendant on an Egypt Air flight that was hijacked on Thanksgiving Weekend, 1985. After watching in horror as four passengers were shot, Jackie realized it was her turn. She was mercilessly shot at point blank range and thrown from the plane onto the tarmac. Altogether, 59 innocent people died during that ordeal. Jackie miraculously lived.

I still remember the part of her speech that really touched me. She said that several years after that traumatic experience, while still struggling with bitterness and negativity, she gave herself the gift of forgiveness. I loved the wording of that – and the meaning behind it! She gave *herself* the gift of forgiveness.

Can you forgive others? I mean, there's so much they have done to us! In their book *Yes, You Can!* Sam Deep and Lyle Sussman write: "At some point I must give up hopes for a better yesterday." We've all had people who have wronged us. But if we just keep wishing for a better yesterday, we'll stay in torment. Forgiveness is what allows us to truly let go.

Oh, and while we're talking about forgiving others, may I also invite you to forgive yourself?

"The ineffable joy of forgiving and being forgiven forms an ecstasy that might well arouse the envy of the gods."

—*Elbert Hubbard*

Give yourself a priceless gift by completing this sentence aloud: "Today I choose to forgive_____." And then do it.

To Be
or
Not To Be

Torch Tip #5
Be wholehearted.

"The antidote to exhaustion may not be rest;
it may be wholeheartedness."

– David Steindl-Rast

I know many halfhearted people, but I don't hang out with them. They are tired, weary people. Their energy levels are dangerously low. Consequently, they drain energy from all available sources, including you and me.

On the other hand, people who are wholehearted are so vivacious, enthusiastic, and full of life. Their energy is a positive force. When I am with them, my torch burns brighter. Interestingly, my wholehearted friends are also my most successful friends. Hmmm...

When I am fully engaged, my creativity peaks. Synchronicity abounds. Depression is chased away. Production skyrockets. Quality improves. Time flies. Sensitivity heightens. And I am happiest.

Whatever you do, just do it with all your heart. We've been given the gift of life! Celebrate! I was an adult before I realized that life is not a dress rehearsal – this is it! Why do anything halfheartedly?

And I love this sentiment from Joan Baez: "You don't get to choose how you're going to die, or when. You can only decide how you are going to live, now."

Be wholehearted!

"The cure for boredom is not diversion;
it is to find some work to do;
it's to find something to care about."

—John Gardner

- I N V I T A T I O N -

Who is your most "wholehearted" friend?
Interview her on this subject to gain insight and motivation.

Torch Tip #6
Be grateful.

"Gratitude is the heart's memory."

– French Proverb

For me, gratefulness is spiritual Prozac. I mean, I think it's nearly impossible to be depressed when we're busy being grateful. What is depression if not repressed anger? Gratitude extinguishes anger...and fuels the fire in that torch of yours.

Gratefulness has often been a key element in my speeches for various companies. I ask employees to think about being grateful for where they live, what they do, and whom they serve. Yes, whom they serve!

I now live in Southern California, and if you've known me for more than five minutes or so, you will have heard me rave about how beautiful it is here. I always say, "Los Angeles is the best place I've ever lived!" One time my wife reminded me that I've said that about *all* the places we've lived...Boston, London, Phoenix, and Atlanta. I guess I've been purposely looking for the positives, no matter where I am.

Be grateful for your family and friends, for your job and co-workers, and for where you live. Thank people who have helped you, and give credit to others when it's appropriate (and, by the way, it's *always* appropriate). Be grateful for your pets! Be grateful for a good movie on a rainy day. Be grateful for a good roof on a rainy day. Be grateful for rain...

...Be grateful.

"What a wonderful life I've had!
I only wish I'd realized it sooner."

—*Colette*

- I N V I T A T I O N -

Write down three things you too often take for granted.

1. _____

2. _____

3. _____

Torch Tip #7
Be a servant.

"I don't know what your destiny will be,
but one thing I do know...The ones amongst you
who are really happy are those who have sought
and found how to serve."

– *Dr. Albert Schweitzer*

Now that we're determined to be grateful, here's a fantastic way to show it: Be a servant. That may mean something as simple as getting your spouse a cup of coffee or buying your co-worker a Coke. Don't ask "How much will this inconvenience me?" Instead, ask "How important is it to them?"

One of my friends was having marriage difficulties. Separation seemed imminent. I asked, "What do you want from your marriage?"

He replied, "I want to make it work. What do you suggest I do?"

I offered this most important question: "What is the one thing you could do tonight that would absolutely shock her with glee?"

Without even a blink, he chimed, "Oh, probably cleaning the toilets."

"Well, there it is, my friend. There's the solution."

With a disgruntled look, he complained, "What do you think I am – a servant?"

I mused, "Now you're getting it."

He did not clean that toilet.

"It just didn't ring true for me," he later told me.

By the way, they're now divorced.

Perhaps there is no nobler position. Be a servant.

> *"I slept and dreamt that life was joy;*
> *I awoke and saw that life was service;*
> *I acted and behold, service was joy."*
>
> *– Rabindranath Tagore*

- I N V I T A T I O N -

Serve someone today. Do likewise tomorrow.

Torch Tip #8
Be yourself.

"Most people are other people...their thoughts are someone else's opinions...their lives a mimicry...their passions a quotation."

– Oscar Wilde

This torch tip is very dear to my heart. I don't even like the word "conformity." In fact, I despise it. And yet it's rampant. I think it starts in our school systems. We seem to have it on straight at the preschool and kindergarten levels. Children come in, they have fun. They eat snacks. You get to sit wherever you want on the floor. Little bit tired after lunch? That's fine! Lie down, take a nap. Listen to stories? Play time? What fun!

It was in such a flexible, dynamic environment that some of the most eager learning of my life occurred. Hmmm...

When we get to first grade, the change begins. "Enough individualism," I believe they're saying. "It's time to conform!"

We now must sit in our chairs.

The chairs are in rows...and every room looks the same.

The conformity has begun.

A child laments, "No nap time now?"
"No, just pay attention and sit up straight in your chair!"

"No, you may not go to the bathroom without a lavatory pass!"

It goes on.

"Did I hear someone speaking or whispering? You don't speak in this class without permission."

"Who brought these crayons? *This is no place for crayons.* You should have outgrown them by now. And by the way, the only pencils you'll use are #2 pencils!"

(I don't even see #1 pencils in the stores – I think they've actually been discontinued due to all this conformity!)

We're not all #2 pencils.

No wonder Neil Postman wrote: "Children enter school as question marks and leave as periods."

In his inspiring book *The Four Agreements*, Don Miguel Ruiz concludes: "All our normal tendencies are lost in the process... We create an image of how we should be in order to be accepted by everybody."

Be yourself, my friends.

"A man must consider what a rich realm he abdicates when he becomes a conformist."

—*Ralph Waldo Emerson*

– I N V I T A T I O N –

The next time you witness a child expressing his individuality, praise him!

Torch Tip #9
Be in awe.

"Sell your cleverness, and purchase bewilderment."

– Rumi

I have never cared for the saying, "Been there; done that; bought the T-shirt." It never struck me as funny. And, sadly, people who live their lives that way rarely even smile.

Albert Einstein once shared, "There are two ways to live your life. One is as though nothing is a miracle. The other is as though everything is a miracle." Frankly, "miraculous" living makes be smile.

While living in Arizona, I delighted in taking my visiting friends to one of the Seven Natural Wonders of the World, the immense Grand Canyon. One week I had the privilege of taking two of my closer friends. One of them was wide-eyed with amazement, while the other seemed nonchalant.

Imagine you are on that trip with us, right now. Listen to my friends' comments and notice your reaction.

"Wow! This is spectacular!"
"Yeah, it's OK, I guess."

"I have never seen anything like this!"
"The Hawaiian island of Kauai also has a grand canyon. I saw it a few years ago."

A sense of awe not only energizes you, it does the same for those around you. After that trip, I have always felt a bit closer to my friend who has chosen to be "in awe."

"Now I can wake up and say, 'Good morning, God!'
rather than 'Good God, it's morning!'"

— Anonymous

– I N V I T A T I O N –

Keep an "Awe Journal." Make at least one entry every day.

In Joy

Torch Tip #10
Enjoy a fine dining experience.

"Life is a banquet...and most of us are starving to death."

– Auntie Mame

I was in Orlando, Florida on a business trip, and things were not going well. I really had not achieved my objectives. I was away from my wife and my daughters. And I was feeling a bit lonely and down.

While sitting in my hotel room, I scanned the room service menu contemplating what to eat. As a professional speaker traveling the country, I've done this more times than I care to count. As I picked up the phone to order, I remembered when checking in I had seen a restaurant called Shula's Steak House. Shula's is, of course, named after Don Shula, the famous football coach for the Miami Dolphins. I'd read in an airline magazine that this restaurant was exceptional. I hesitated, as I rarely dine at such a nice place. But that night, I thought, I'm going to treat myself.

I strolled into Shula's, and held up one finger – "Party of one, please." From the moment I walked in, I didn't feel alone anymore. The customer service was phenomenal! Everyone was courteous, attentive and smiling. The menu was even shaped like a football. They brought out an impressive platter of meat so I could choose what I wanted before they cooked it. I selected a succulent rib eye.

My dining experience was exceptional! Upon my return to the hotel room, I actually felt much better! I *had* accomplished some positive things on this trip, and I *could* catch up on those remaining objectives tomorrow.

So I would remember this experience, I scribbled on a sheet of hotel stationery:

Occasionally, whether you can afford it or not, enjoy a fine dining experience.

– I N V I T A T I O N –

For a treat, ask a friend out to a special dinner.

Torch Tip #11
Enjoy your work.

"Choose a job you love, and you will never
have to work a day in your life."

– Confucius

I once read an article entitled "Top 4 Reasons to Change Jobs."
They were:

1. You dread going to work.
2. You live only for the weekends.
3. You no longer take pride in your work.
4. You've lost your sense of humor.

Not long after reading this, I was invited to speak to a
work team of eighty. The director explained to me that they
had lost seven employees in the past two weeks. She was
concerned and was hoping I could say something to stop
the exodus. You should have seen her face when, instead,
I read the article!

She called me three hours later. Frustrated, she told me she
had received nine more notices to quit! I explained that
these decisions would probably benefit her remaining team,
her customers, and perhaps even those who had departed.
After some thought, she agreed.

My friend, do you enjoy your work?

Perhaps you feel trapped. It may feel like you don't have
choices, but you do! Take action. See if your company is
hiring in another department, or perhaps start looking for
a job somewhere else.

But please don't walk around saying, "I want to go home... I don't want to be here... I'm so glad it's Friday... The weekend was too short..."

You deserve better. And so do your co-workers.

"At the end of 20 years, you can have 20 years' experience, or one year's experience 20 times. It's your choice."

– Richard Gilly Nixon

– I N V I T A T I O N –

Find creative ways to enjoy your work, or change your work!

Torch Tip #12
Enjoy nature.

"In all things of nature there is something of the marvelous."
– Aristotle

My daughter couldn't believe there wasn't a TV in the room.
I opened the door and showed her the sky and the ocean...
the breathtaking majesty of Big Sur, California. I turned to
her and said: "Today, let's tune in to *this* program."

No place recharges me like Big Sur. Just south of Monterey
on Highway 1, Big Sur is a nonstop awe-inspiring, panoramic
sanctuary of granite cliffs, divine ocean vistas, grassy mead-
ows, and majestic redwood forests. Hike Pfeiffer Falls Trail,
and eat a picnic lunch beside a 60-foot waterfall. If that
waterfall isn't big enough for you, a little to the south you'll
discover the picturesque McWay Falls – this diamond of
nature brilliantly cascades down a towering 80-foot cliff
onto an exquisite, pristine beach.

This is where I go to get rejuvenated, replenished, and
re-energized. And driving there is just as invigorating as
being there. Even as I get in the car and pull out of my
driveway, I'm already starting to breathe more slowly and
deeply. It's such a metaphor for "Life is in the journey."

Of course, Big Sur has its share of award-winning pricier
escapes, like the rustic luxury of the Post Ranch Inn or the
Ventana Inn and Spa. I have yet to experience those. I stay
in the more affordable campsites or retreat centers, such
as Big Sur Campground, the Esalen Institute, or the
Growing Edge Center for Sustainable Peace and Healing.
"Sustainable Peace and Healing" – I love that.

Find your place; the place that rejuvenates you. It might be a drive up the coast, a canoe trip down a river, or a hike up a hill or mountain; it might even be in your backyard hammock!

"I believe in God, only I spell it Nature."

— Frank Lloyd Wright

– I N V I T A T I O N –

Visit one of Mother Nature's own
"Centers for Sustainable Peace and Healing" near you!

Torch Tip #13
Enjoy some company – yours.

"Conversation enriches the understanding,
but solitude is the school of genius."

– Sir Edward Gibbon

That's right. Spend some time with yourself – alone. I've read that many people believe that how you feel about being alone is a direct reflection of your self-esteem. I mean if we really don't like spending time with ourselves, how can we expect others to love being with us?

How do you feel about being alone?

I never spent much time alone, until I moved to California. As I just shared with you, I found the magic of Big Sur. I started going for two- or three-night stays. At first it was so strange being alone and not speaking to others! But I was OK, as long as I had my music with me.

One day my friend Carl Patterson invited me to leave my music at home. He enticed, "Wonderful things may happen when there are fewer distractions."

...*Wonderful?* This was anything *but* wonderful. For the first eight hours, I didn't know what to do with myself. No one to talk to; no TV nor radio or phone, no computer nor e-mail... and *no music. Just me!*

Thanks, Carl (dripping with sarcasm)!

As evening drew near, it finally happened. A reprieve. Something just clicked, and I actually started enjoying those moments. I attained a deeper level of thinking than I ever had before.

When you're in a still place, and you're steeped in silence, positive things happen. You get to know yourself. I highly recommend this adventure, my friends.

At first my family didn't understand it. They thought I was selfish. "What do you mean, you're going away alone, Dad?" And my wife was suspicious: "Do you have a woman up there?" No. I was just learning to enjoy my own company. And the way it rekindled my spirit and invigorated me was incredible!

I now go away for "My Weekend" about once every three months. I love this time; I yearn for it.

And by the way, my children and my wife no longer question my going...they urge me! Especially when I'm getting a little stressed or short-tempered, they now say, "Isn't it about time you take off for one of your weekends?" They know that I need this invaluable time; and I think that maybe we all do. It took me 45 years to understand this. I assure you, it'll improve your relationships and your outlook – and it'll add fuel to your fire.

Thanks, Carl (dripping with gratitude)!

"It doesn't interest me where or what or with whom you have studied. I want to know what sustains you, from the inside, when all else falls away. I want to know if you can be alone with yourself and if you truly like the company you keep in the empty moments."

– Oriah Mountain Dreamer

– INVITATION –

Take time to be alone today.
Start small (a bath, a walk, a sit in the park).
Plan a longer excursion.

Word Play

Read

"In the case of good books, the point is not to see how many you can get through, but rather how many can get through to you."

— Mortimer Jerome Adler

It's amazing to hear myself say this...I spent so much of my life not reading.

A group of my co-workers would take off for lunch once a week and not invite me. One day I finally asked my friend Mark, "Where do you guys go when I'm not invited?" He told me that they go to a book club. A little upset, I asked, "So why don't you invite me?" Mark looked right at me and deadpanned: "Because you don't read."

Sometimes it's hard to hear the truth...it was so good for me, though. It opened the door to a whole world I hadn't yet experienced. I started reading more and more. Now I can't get enough of it!

Thanks, Mark!

And reading doesn't have to be an expensive passion. Simply stated, library cards are too rare a possession these days. And here are a few additional ways I discovered I could read at very little cost.

First, I started downgrading the delivery cost when I ordered books on Amazon.com. It took three long weeks for the books to arrive, but that was fine since I had plenty already in stock.

Then I found the joy of *used* books – I was buying books for 2 to 5 dollars each.

Later, a friend shared his secret for getting the biggest amount of books for his buck: Yard sales! I was in literary – and financial – heaven.

But my latest scheme tops them all: I find fantastic books for less than 75 cents each. How? I order them from eBay – used books, and only in *bulk*.

I had 200 books arrive at my home last month!

I try to read a couple of books each week. And by the way, I love the notes and the highlighted portions from past readers! I think books should be worth even more if they've been highlighted and marked.

Read newspapers from other cities! Read Shakespeare. There's a reason he's the only author with his own section in the bookstore...well, along with Dan Brown and J.K. Rowling.

If you're not sure what you want to read, you can see what's popular by perusing the best seller lists on Amazon.com or BarnesandNoble.com. There are also Web sites where you can look up the winners of the Nobel Prize for Literature, the Pulitzer Prize, and the National Book Award.

> *"Reading is equivalent to thinking with someone else's head, instead of your own."*
>
> *– Arthur Schopenhauer*

– INVITATION –

Why not begin reading that book you've been thinking about?

Torch Tip #15
Poetry

"Poetry is the language in which man explores
his own amazement."

— Christopher Fry

I can assure you, my friends, if you get involved with poetry at any level, there will be a significant increase in the brightness of your torch. And I recently heard that reading and listening to poetry harmonizes breathing, reduces stress, and actually slows down the heart rate!

Looking for a poetic place to start? Go to the American Academy of Poets Web site at www.poets.org. Or just find the poetry section in your local bookstore.

I invite you to be inspired by one of my favorite poems:

Come to the Edge

"Come to the edge," he said.
They said, "We are afraid."
"Come to the edge," he said.
They came.
He pushed them...
...and they flew.

— Guillaume Apollinaire

Poetry. Write it, read it, listen to it, memorize it, and be amazed by it.

"Any healthy man can go without food for two days — but not without poetry."

— Charles Baudelaire

Display your favorite poem where it can inspire you.

Torch Tip #16
Quotes

*"Quotations, when engraved upon the memory,
give you good thoughts."*

— Sir Winston Churchill

As you see, included in this book are some of my very
favorite quotes, and I'm always looking for more. To me,
quotes are just condensed wisdom.

As a bonus, I have included in the back of this book more of
my favorite motivational quotes. Feel free to add your own.

George Bernard Shaw, the author of the quote that inspired
this book, quips: "I often quote myself; it adds spice to my
conversation."

Get a quote book, highlight the ones you like, and then
memorize them. It adds fuel to your fire, my friend. Here's
another idea: Make a quote book for someone you love.
E-mail a relevant quote to someone...you know, something
that speaks to what they're going through at the time. Tear
out a quote from a calendar or magazine, and give it to
someone you care about.

You can find a fantastic collection of quotes on
www.bartleby.com or www.quotationspage.com.

Quotes – read them, study them, and memorize them.

"I quote others; only the better to express myself."

— Michel de Montaigne

Memorize your favorite three quotes.

Write

"We are cups, constantly and quietly being filled.
The trick is, knowing how to tip ourselves over
and let the beautiful stuff out."

– Ray Bradbury

It's time to start writing! Journals. Diaries. Letters. Books.
Articles. Short stories. Songs. Screenplays. It's up to you
what you write, but *just begin!* It's so exhilarating to get your
thoughts down on paper (or onto a computer screen).

Need a little inspiration? A jumpstart? Read Anne Lamott's
hilarious *Bird by Bird: Some Instructions on Writing and Life.*
It's one of my favorites and the consummate how-to/why-to
guide for new writers.

Or feel like you have writer's block? Take a walk. To get the
creative juices flowing, Raymond Inmon shares, "Angels
whisper to a man when he goes for a walk."

While you write, you'll notice that your thoughts will clarify.
Find out about writing groups, courses, or conferences in
your area. Or just take a few quiet moments, maybe at the
beginning or end of the day, to write – I think you'll find it
peaceful and fulfilling.

"There are a thousand thoughts lying within a man
that he does not know till he takes up a pen to write."

– William Makepeace Thackeray

– INVITATION –

*I have always believed that
every person has a book inside of her.
What is the title of yours?*

_____

Torch Tip #18
Passwords

*"Handle them carefully, for words
have more power than atom bombs."*

– Pearl Strachan

Take advantage of the power found in words.

I admit this is kind of a strange tip. But I started realizing that in today's society of technology, I probably have 30 different passwords. You know, there's one for the mainframe, one for each e-mail account, one for eBay, one for home, one for work, *ad infinitum.*

How can we turn this frustration into a positive experience?

What if we use unique passwords – words that convey caring or generate positive energy every time we "log in"?

You can have some fun thinking up your own. Here are some of mine.

Thinner...Celebrate...Empower...Dazzle...Powerful...Smile... Loving.

It's so positive just to sort through these words!

Honoring...Peaceful...Passion...Amazing...Grateful.

Oh, and please don't use this information to log in to my eBay account!

*"Words are, of course, the most
powerful drug used by mankind."*

– Rudyard Kipling

Have fun choosing your own powerful passwords.
Jot down a few below.

Ixnay

Torch Tip #19
Avoid addictions.

*"First you take a drink, then the drink takes a drink,
then the drink takes you."*

– Francis Scott Key Fitzgerald

Addictions distract us from finding our goals. Addictions prevent us from fulfilling our purpose. Addictions disturb friendships and marriages. Food, drugs, drinking, shopping. Some people are addicted to suffering. You can even be addicted to another person. In *The Power of Now*, Eckhart Tolle says that you have an addiction if "you no longer feel that you have the choice to stop." Get help if needed, and do all you can to avoid those addictions.

Let me confess something to you. Starting way back when I was in college, I tried marijuana. I didn't just try it once or twice. For years and years, I smoked. And unlike a certain past President, I inhaled (in fact, some of my friends wondered if I ever exhaled)!

If I hadn't dealt with that addiction, I don't think I ever would've written my books, recorded my CDs, started my own company, or formed good relationships with my family and friends.

Today, I struggle with the addiction of food. Though not illegal, it is as serious as any drug or alcohol problem. It has already affected my health, and my self-esteem. The battle rages.

Work hard to avoid addictions.

*"Why do human beings acquire bad habits so easily?
... The white man and the red man came face to face
at a crucial juncture in history, and the first thing they
did was exchange vices (tobacco vs. alcohol)."*

—*Ralph Cinque*

– INVITATION –

*Do you have an addiction that's smothering your flame?
Can you give it up for one day...then maybe another?*

Stay out of debt.

"Golden shackles are far worse than iron ones."

– Mahatma Gandhi

"We spend a lot of time...we don't have,
doing things...we don't enjoy,
in places...we don't prefer,
to buy things...we don't need,
with money...we don't have,
to impress people...we don't like."

– compilation of my quote and others

I have a friend in Atlanta named Alex. He's a successful, brilliant man. Alex is 40 years old, and he's already paid off his home. He has no car payments and no credit card payments. And let me tell you, he lives just a bit more vivaciously than most. His fire is burning! Stay debt-free!

*"Another way to solve the traffic problems
of this country is to pass a law that only paid-for cars
be allowed to use the highways."*

– Will Rogers

Though this is obviously a tongue-in-cheek quip, this Rogers quote may challenge many of us readers. Not only are autos a depreciation pit, through steep interest payments they also hamper our financial freedom. Too often, consumers buy cars based on the maximum payment for which they qualify, rather than on the most dependable transportation for the most affordable rate.

I've found through personal experience that when you have debt, it will weigh heavily on your spirit. I've had times in my life when people were calling our home to collect money we didn't have to send them. That debt robbed me of my passion and extinguished my creativity, not to mention the limits it put on my generosity.

Don't allow debt to douse your torch.

"Money talks...but all mine ever says is good-bye."

— Anonymous

– INVITATION –

Begin dreaming and scheming of ways to become debt-free.

Torch Tip #21
Abhor average.

"If you deliberately plan on being less than you are capable of being, then I warn you that you'll be unhappy for the rest of your life."

– Abraham H. Maslow

Friend, boxer, minister, and real estate developer Chris McGrath writes:

"Average is
> the top of the bottom...
> the best of the worst...
> the bottom of the top...
> the worst of the best...

> The saddest epitaph is this: 'Here lies Mr. Average. Here lies the remains of what might have been, except for his belief that he was only average.'"

When I first met Chris, he was, by his own account, an average speaker. He had limited education and no presentation experience. He was determined to improve and was willing to go to any lengths to do so. He watched other speakers, always taking notes. He asked for feedback after his sermons. Many nights I remember Chris, in my garage, practicing his upcoming sermons. Using my ironing board as his pulpit, he enthusiastically spoke to an audience of one. When he had finished, I would offer suggestions. After a few moments of scribbling, he would begin again...and again.

Chris became a powerful and polished presenter! Having ministered churches on many continents, he has spoken all over the world. Today, he is a favorite of many, including myself...and there is nothing average about him.

"The road to happiness lies in two simple principles: find what interests you and that you can do well, and put your whole soul into it — every bit of energy and ambition and natural ability you have."

— John D. Rockefeller III

– I N V I T A T I O N –

Think of one aspect of your life where your performance may be average.
Now think of the benefits of improving that area.

Torch Tip #22
Control your temper.

"When anger rises, think of the consequences."

– Confucius

Grown adults still lose their tempers. Next time you hear someone say they have a terrible temper, say: "I'm sorry to hear that." There's nothing amusing about a lost temper – and there can be a whole lot of harm. Lost tempers frighten children. Lost tempers cause broken hearts. Lost tempers cause domestic violence. Lost tempers cause road rage. Control your temper.

I still remember an incident – a vacation I was on with my wife and two daughters. It was a Northwest flight, and we were in the airport in Minneapolis. And it all started because of something so silly.

My wife was asking the flight attendant if we should change our money into pounds in the airport, or wait until we arrived in England. And this flight attendant, who regularly flew to England, gave his answer, and I disagreed with it. I said, "No, it's better to do it the other way." He then bristled and shot back with sarcasm, "I *think* I would know…I've been flying there for 10 years." With my voice rivaling the sound of the jets taking off, I then rebutted, "Well, I *lived* there for 8 years! So maybe it's time you keep your nose out of our business!"

And it got even worse.

I remember glancing over at my daughters who were so embarrassed to be sitting there. They still recall the time

I lost my temper in the airport on our way to England. I think that flight attendant probably still remembers as well. I know that I'm still embarrassed.

"The worst tempered people I've ever met were people who knew they were wrong."

—*Wilson Mizner*

- INVITATION -

Please join me in my resolve to avoid this poisonous practice.

Don't complain.

*"There are persons who always find a hair
in their plate of soup for the simple reason that,
when they sit down before it, they shake their
heads until one falls in."*

— Friedrich Hebbel

No one likes a whiner. And there's just no reason for it.

We've all been there. You're out eating with friends, and you hear:

> "Oh, this place is always crowded."
> "I hate waiting in line."
> "I *told* you we should've gone somewhere else."
> "Oh great, we get *this* table. I bet it'll be noisy."

It continues:

> "This silverware is dirty."
> "The last time I had the steak it was too well done."
> "Do you feel a draft in here?"

On and on it goes. And bite by bite, your food loses its taste.

If you just recognized yourself, it's time to repent...or eat alone.

No one likes a complainer.

*"Don't complain. The wheel that squeaks
the loudest often gets replaced."*

— Unknown author

Take the complaining test.
Count how many times you complain in one day.
The next day, reduce the number.
Continue the process.

Treasure Hunt

Torch Tip #24
Find your strengths.

"You will recognize your own path when you come upon it, because you will suddenly have all the energy and imagination you will ever need."

— Jerry Gilles

Find your strengths, and exploit them...find your weaknesses, and don't devote much time correcting them or building them up. For some reason, we seem to do just the opposite. Most of the time, we ignore our strengths and work overtime to improve our weaknesses.

I once worked for a *Fortune 40 Company* that graciously allotted me a yearly educational stipend. I was then encouraged to get training in an area of weakness. And every year I politely declined and chose instead to focus on my strength – speaking. Year after year I decided against instructional design, consultant skills, and process improvement. Like a laser, I honed in on presentation skills. I finally left Corporate America at age 50. I was competent in only one area, and that was enough.

An enlightening book has been written on this subject of focusing on your strengths. *Now, Discover Your Strengths,* by Marcus Buckingham and Donald Clifton, has been on best-seller lists for months, and I wholeheartedly recommend it.

In this book, the authors paint the following scenario:

A child comes home from school with a report card...we check it out:

```
Art     ---- A
English ---- A
Science ---- A
Algebra ---- C
```

What's the parent's next comment going to be? And where's the focus going to be over the next six months? Art? English? Science?

Probably not. Usually the attention goes to improving that Algebra grade...

"What can we do to raise that grade? We'll hire an Algebra tutor for two hours every night."

"But I don't like Algebra, Dad."

"Doesn't matter. You must get better at it. It's your weakness."

What would happen if we brought in the tutor to help this young man further explore and develop his interest in Art, English, or Science? Who knows what future Picasso or Dickenson remains undiscovered?

So, my friend, ignite your torch by exploiting and nourishing your strengths. Bask in your uniqueness...in this, your success will assuredly come.

"When love and skill work together, expect a masterpiece."

– John Ruskin

– I N V I T A T I O N –

Buy the book mentioned above, take the enclosed Clifton StrengthFinder Profile, and brighten your torch!

Torch Tip #25
Find someone who inspires you.

*"Only passions, great passions,
can elevate the soul to great things."*

– Denis Diderot

Please allow me to introduce to you the fascinating Marta Becket.

In the 1960s when Marta was in her mid-40s, she should have been making her final concert tour and concluding her dancing career. Instead, when she and her husband Tom had a flat tire near the ghost town of Death Valley Junction, California (population 10), she discovered an old abandoned theatre and immediately became inspired.

She never left.

After years of renovating and rehearsing, the doors were opened. Marta committed to performing her show *whether or not* people attended. With the nearest town more than 25 miles away, some evenings the only admirers of her craft were the spectacular life-sized figures in the audience murals she had painted on the walls.

She kept dancing.

A few years later, her husband left her to return to New York.

She kept dancing.

At the time of this writing, Marta is 82 years old.

She is still dancing.

Nearly every show is a sellout.

Talk about living your passion!

"Long before anybody invented the term 'performance art,'
Marta Becket was doing it, in an abandoned opera house in
Death Valley Junction. She restored it, and it restored her."

– Jay Carr

I keep a picture of Marta in my office. Every glance at her awakens me and elicits a surge of passion. She is my Muse.

Now *she* restores *me*.

Who's your inspiration? If no one, then find someone.

And set *your* soul on fire!

Then *you* may become *someone else's* inspiration!

- I N V I T A T I O N -

A Night of Inspiration

with

Marta Becket

Where: Amargosa Opera House
Admission: $15
Open: October–May
Phone: (760) 852-4441
E-mail: amargosaoperahouse.com

Torch Tip #26
Find the best in others.

"There is no object so foul that intense light will not make it beautiful."

– Ralph Waldo Emerson

If we have a hard time finding the best in someone, maybe we need to shed more light on them.

Be relentless in this quest. Refuse to focus on the negatives! I promise that this will transform your relationships. I make a conscious effort every day to look for the best in other people. Granted, for some it's easier than others.

About a year ago, I was recommending someone for a corporate project. I kept praising her, "She'd be great for that position. She's friendly, she's kind, and she's intelligent..."

Her boss stopped me and said, "James, she's only that way with you."

I started thinking about her comment. Was that true? Why? Maybe it's because I always want to find the best in others. Maybe that's why they're being their best when I'm with them.

So, let's find the best in others.

And while we're at it, let's also try to find the best in ourselves.

"We awaken in others the same attitude of mind we hold toward them."

—Elbert Hubbard

– INVITATION –

Tomorrow, search for the best in everyone you see.
Begin at home.

Torch Tip #27
Find a way to make someone's day.

"We get to make a living; we give to make a life."

– Sir Winston Churchill

My family and I were on a vacation – our first boat cruise. From Los Angeles, you can go on a three-day cruise fairly inexpensively. Our ship stopped in Ensenada, Mexico, where we disembarked and hopped on the free cruise-shuttle tour to the city center, enjoying sights along the way.

When it was time to go back to the ship, we took a taxi which had seen many better days in its apparent 20 years of service. Poverty was all around us along this quicker return route. But I remember that our driver was so incredibly nice to us. He taught the girls some Spanish, and he even took our picture upon our arrival at the dock. The fare was $5, so I gave him $7.

As soon as he drove off, my older daughter, Alexandra, asked, "Dad, why didn't you give the cab driver $10?"

And I started explaining, "Honey, the fare was only $5, and I gave him $7 – that's a 40-percent tip! And you saw how grateful he was."

She acknowledged, "Yes, I saw him smile, but anytime you can make someone's day for $5, shouldn't you do that?"

I was dumbfounded. She was right. I've never forgotten that.

Thank you, Alexandra.

"You have not lived today until you have done something for someone who can never repay you."

— John Bunyon

Find a way to make someone's day for $5.

Visiting Hours

Visit a third world country.

"Abundance is not something we acquire.
It is something we tune into."

– Dr. Wayne Dyer

You want your torch to burn a little brighter?

See how the rest of the world lives. Visit a third world country. And don't just go with a compassionate attitude. Go also with the idea: *What can I learn from them?*

I've had the opportunity in my life to visit several countries that would be considered in this "third world" category. I think the ones most notable in my mind were in West Africa, the countries of Ghana and Nigeria. And in Asia, India was a definite. I now live in Southern California and you don't even have to cross an ocean to find third world poverty. Cross the border into Tijuana, and I think you'll see what I mean.

If you go to one of these countries, take your children. Let them collect some toys and clothes of theirs and of neighborhood friends to give to the children in the country you'll be visiting. I promise you, this will forever impact your life – and the lives of your children.

And while you're in that third world country, make it a point to visit a local hospital. I'll never forget the one that Tanya and I visited in Ghana. What we saw there is still sharply embedded in our minds.

We complain about things in our hospitals:
"The air conditioning is too cold."

"The food isn't hot enough."

"She has to share her room with three other patients."

"I rang this buzzer, and it took a nurse two minutes to get here!"

Our visit to that Ghanaian hospital was a convicting contrast where cold air, cold food, a nurse's visit, or just a bed would have been a very welcomed blessing.

As Tanya and I approached the hospital's entrance, we curiously walked past dozens of people sitting amongst a motley patchwork of torn towels and rags strewn across the entire dirt "front lawn." Any available bush or branch was similarly adorned.

As we began walking around inside, our hearts just broke. The very rare patient with a bed and mattress was the extremely fortunate one. Most had just bed springs. Some patients were even lying on the floor. And each person had just a ragged cloth beneath them.

As we glanced through a broken window at that sea of towels and rags outside, we were humbled to realize that all those precious scraps of cloth *were* their pillows, mattresses, sheets, covers, washcloths, and towels which the families themselves supplied, washed, and "sun-dried" for their loved ones.

We just wanted to cry... for them... for their conditions... for their lot in life.

But we couldn't. Not then, anyway. We were there to visit and encourage.

Yet, most amazingly, it was Tanya and I who became encouraged. Astoundingly, there were smiles everywhere – on the faces of nurses, doctors, visiting family, and even on the faces of the sick and dying. They were so *grateful* someone came to visit and just share a friendly smile or gentle touch. Many visitors got up off the floor (there were no chairs) and hugged us. Just so *appreciative* someone cared. I'll never forget it. What grateful and *good* people!

We cried for that... after we left.

And these are the people often referred to as *underdeveloped*.

> *"Lives based on having are less free than lives based on either doing or being."*
>
> — *William James*

– I N V I T A T I O N –

Visit a third world country, whether in person, in books, or through the Internet.

Visit a prison.

"Nothing could blot out the knowledge of what and where you were...or the certainty that this was all that life held for you."

– Alcatraz prisoner #AZ586

I had the opportunity to visit San Francisco with my younger daughter, Natasha. She was so excited about going over to Alcatraz. But something strange happened that day. As our tour boat slowly drifted to dock at Alcatraz, an uneasy feeling came over me. It was powerful enough for me to stop my conversation with my daughter. It's difficult to articulate, but of this I am sure: Dread, sadness, and hopelessness hover around that fortress. When I saw those prison cells, I just couldn't shake the feeling of despair. Imagine being told when to sleep, when to wake up, when to eat, and even who can visit. Imagine being controlled so completely for all those years.

When I read Dante's *Inferno*, one line shook me sober. It was the greeting on the archway to Hell: "All ye who enter here, leave all hope behind."

Prisons are horrible places. They squash freedom and hope. Can you imagine ever *volunteering* to serve a prison sentence? Millions of people do – in their own minds.

We "sentence" ourselves with limiting beliefs:

"I'm stuck in a job I hate."
"I could never learn that skill."

"I've given up on love."
"I'll always be overweight."

Amazingly, to escape from these internal prisons, all that's required of us is a decision – a shift in perception. Don't leave hope behind, my friend. Unlock the door to possibilities in your life!

"Man is free at the moment he wishes to be."

– Voltaire

– INVITATION –

What prison bars have you built around yourself?
You alone have the key to freedom.
Ready to break out?

Torch Tip #30
Visit a graveyard.

*"Once the game is over, the king and the pawn
go back in the same box."*

– Italian Proverb

Are you ready to leave this earth? Does work or life's responsibilities just seem too overwhelming at times?

Have I got the antidote for you: Visit a graveyard.

The day that I wrote this, I was visiting a graveyard in Newburyport, Massachusetts. It was so majestic – huge gravestones and elaborate tombs. But most of all, it was sobering – a solemn guarantee that we're all going to end up there. It certainly was a somber reminder of the brevity of life.

As a child in Raleigh, North Carolina, I remember sitting in the car while my father visited my grandmother's grave. It was an interesting dynamic, watching Dad look at his mother's grave. Then only a few years later, I again stood beside him, looking now at the graves of both his mother and father.

It didn't take me long to paint the picture: One day I'd be looking at my own parents' graves. That day has already happened.

It's not difficult to figure out the natural pattern.

I'm next.

And you know what? This realization does not depress me; it *motivates me* – to get going! I think that any time we get a chance to have a stare-down with our own mortality, our torch burns just a little bit brighter.

"Burn, burn, burn like the fabulous yellow roman candles exploding like spiders across the stars, and in the middle you see the blue center light pop, and everybody goes 'Awww.'"

– *Jack Kerouac*

– I N V I T A T I O N –

What is it you most want to accomplish?
Think about it the next time you drive by a graveyard.

Torch Tip #31
Visit a place that inspires you.

"It's amazing the difference a bit of sky can make."

— Shel Silverstein

You already know that Big Sur is my first choice for inspiration. And yet I'd have to say that Yosemite National Park is a close second. Winter is glorious there, but an early Spring visit just transports me (think maximum waterfalls)!

Another favorite is San Diego, where I've seen ocean waves that actually glow. It's nothing short of spellbinding. When the waves crash, they light up – almost as if they're on fire. Are you lucky enough to live near water? One glimpse of the ocean and I'm a new person.

Art galleries enchant Tanya; museums captivate Alexandra; good musicals impassion Natasha; and attending the 1996 Atlanta Paralympics amazed and uplifted all four of us!

What place emboldens you? Where's your idea of paradise?

Maybe it's your garden or a hiking trail near your home. Or is it a visit to "The Big Apple" or a tour to Rome?

Maybe looking up at the night sky inspires you. I dare anyone to gaze at its beauty and vastness and remain pessimistic. During a meteor shower or lunar eclipse, my friend always heads for the desert, which fascinates him with its exquisite, panoramic views of the heavens.

Visit a place that gives you wonder. Then see how *wonder-full* your life becomes!

*"The richness I achieve comes from Nature,
the source of my inspiration."*

— Claude Monet

- I N V I T A T I O N -

What places inspire you? Is it time for a visit?

Do Unto Others

Torch Tip #32
Cherish your friendships.

"We are each of us angels, with only one wing.
So we can only fly embracing one another."

—*Luciano de Crescenzo*

Even as I wrote this, I felt my torch burn more brilliantly. Make new friends and nurture the old ones. Return that phone call, or better yet, initiate the phone call! Always embrace these sacred bonds.

I'm blessed with awesome friends:

- Charlie, in Denver. He is so encouraging, and he also taught me to live life with a positive attitude.
- Carl, in Raleigh. We played college football together and now trust our deepest secrets with one another.
- Tamara, in San Diego. Being a Wake Forest Alumni, I never thought I would love a graduate from the University of North Carolina, but this woman has had a monumental impact in my life.
- Ron, in Atlanta. He is my mentor in the challenging arenas of integrity, perseverance, and fitness.
- Suzie, my sister, in Concord. She and I share wonderful laughter.

I cherish building a history with someone and developing a true friendship.

I've found that when I want to get together with someone, it works best when we're specific about the details. Instead of "Let's get together soon," how about "Let's see a movie this Saturday afternoon."

And by all means, get up from your desk at work and go chat with someone for five minutes.

It might be the best part of your day – and theirs! And that co-worker might just become a friend.

"Friends are treasures."

– Horace Bruns

- I N V I T A T I O N -

Maybe it's a good time to give a call or write a letter. Let new friends and old friends know how much they mean to you.

Torch Tip #33
Honor everyone.

"How far you go in life depends on your being tender with the young, compassionate with the aged, sympathetic with the striving, and tolerant of the weak and strong, because someday in your life, you will have been all of these."

– George Washington Carver

In Southern California, I've noticed that we have this unusual practice known as "celebrity worship." I really don't get it. We should honor everyone. Yet, people definitely don't get treated the same; not just here in California, but everywhere in the world.

Do you honor everyone?

The bank president and the bank janitor?

The star of the team and the team's trainer?

Do you walk past people who clean the restrooms at your office, treating them like they're invisible? Why don't you smile and say "Hi"? That might just make their day. What a wonderful way to help your torch – and theirs – burn brighter.

I know why this torch tip means so much to me. I was once an evangelist for a dynamic church, and I was treated with incredible respect. After ten years, I stepped down from the ministry and was just a "regular" member of the congregation. And guess what? I was treated differently.

The honor was removed...and it hurt.

Years later I left that church altogether...and once more I was treated in a noticeably different way.

Except by Andy Broughton.

Andy has *always* treated me the same – with kindness and respect – whether in or out of the ministry – whether in or out of his church. This kind man lives in Scotland, and yet for the past decade, he has regularly called Tanya and me, just to encourage us. In fact, he called several times as I was writing this book.

Andy has always honored me...and it feels good.

I will never forget this most important lesson.

Thank you, Andy.

> *"We must build a new world, a far better world –*
> *one in which the eternal dignity of man is respected."*
>
> *– President Harry S. Truman*

– INVITATION –

Who has been your "Andy"? Whisper a prayer of thanks for him. Then call him and whisper "Thank you" to him.

Torch Tip #34
Learn from others.

"The teachers are everywhere, what is needed is a learner."

– Wendell Berry

This tip is unique in that learning from others is serendipity. The payoff is how this activity affects your relationships. People enjoy sharing their thoughts, their knowledge, and their stories. Remember that person who always had to share his knowledge? Do you recall the woman who always corrected others with her facts? The one with whom it was pointless to disagree? I used the words "remember" and "recall" because odds are these are friends of the past. Frankly, no one enjoys being around a know-it-all for very long.

On the contrary, imagine a friend who is interested in your thoughts and insights. Imagine someone who asks you to explain further your comments, and responds:

"That makes really good sense!"

"I have never considered that."

"That is interesting. Please tell me more."

Learning from others is about much more than just acquiring facts. It involves having the humility to put aside our "mental fact sheets" and to open that space for others' ideas. Learning is about honoring others who share new or different viewpoints.

I have discovered that my enemy in this regard is my ego. Sometimes my ego doesn't want to learn. It wants to teach! It wants to share with others how much it knows. My ego wants to correct others to set them straight. When someone disagrees with or questions my viewpoint, I'm quick to challenge, "You want to bet on it?" (How endearing!)

Learn from your friends. Learn from your partner. Learn from your children.

> *"Every man I meet is my superior in some way;*
> *in that I learn from him."*
>
> – *Ralph Waldo Emerson*

– INVITATION –

The next time you are in a conversation with someone, silently ask yourself, "What can I learn from her?"

Torch Tip #35
Love people.

*"Love cures people – both the ones who give it,
and the ones who receive it."*

– Carl Menninger

This tip may help your torch glow more radiantly than any other in this book.

Love people – all people.
Love teenagers!
Love the elderly.
Love complainers.
Love illegal immigrants.
Love drivers who cut you off.
Love crying babies on airplanes.
Love loud cell phone talkers in restaurants.
Love people who are trying to push you away. They're just trying to prove to themselves that they're not lovable – prove them wrong.

Notice I didn't say *tolerate* them...I said *love* them. I abhor the title of Simon Wiesenthal's Museum of Tolerance. Don't get me wrong. I love the concept and what it stands for; I just don't like the title – "Museum of Tolerance." It just doesn't sit right with me. I don't know about you, but I don't want to be *tolerated!* I want to be *loved.* I don't want to tolerate people; I want to *love* them.

Is it enough for you to just be tolerated?

Love people.

"The day will come when, after harnessing space, the winds, the tides and gravitation, we shall harness for God the energies of love. And on that day, for the second time in the history of the world, we shall have discovered fire."

— Pierre Teilhard de Chardin

- I N V I T A T I O N -

Is there someone you have been tolerating? Try loving him.

Torch Tip #36
Respect Vietnam Vets.

"In war, there are no unwounded soldiers."

— José Narosky

One day in Big Sur I began thinking about the Vietnam War. I thought back to the ugly receptions many of the soldiers encountered upon returning home. I was grateful that we now show more support for our soldiers. But somehow, it just didn't seem fair for our Vietnam Vets. I felt inspired and compelled to write the following article, which was later submitted and published in my local paper.

I am as proud of this message as any in this book.

I am not saying we shouldn't respect all Veterans. I am saying we should give special attention, respect, and honor to the brave who served their country but were never properly welcomed home.

Where Was the Parade?

I am rarely ashamed of my national heritage. I am an American — and proud of it. The recent Olympics seem to have a way of bolstering my pride, as did a recent article in the newspaper — a "gold medal" story. You probably heard about it. As uniformed American soldiers boarded a commercial flight, a single applause erupted into an entire chorus of patriotic thanks. That, by itself, is a cool story. But what followed really warmed my heart. One by one, first class passengers relinquished their cherished seats to the soldiers. This is among my favorite stories of 2004.

But I am as bothered as I am proud. I just turned 50 this month, and my generation includes the Vietnam Vets. I was not "called," but I knew many who were. Where were the patriotic thanks when they returned?

Where was the parade?

Instead of being "upgraded" at airports, soldiers were "downgraded," as shouts of "Baby killer!" greeted them. Some even had blood tossed on them. Armless and legless, they came home carrying inside them shrapnel, diseases, addictions, and painful memories.

Wounded – body, mind, and soul.

And for the most part – they were deserted. Deserted by the very country for which they risked their lives.

I just learned that over 30% of the homeless in the United States are Vietnam Vets. I am ashamed...are you?

These soldiers also deserve honor and respect. My God – many of them were drafted!

Reparations? I'm all for it. And I bet most Americans would agree. I would gladly contribute to this fund. Fresh starts, homes for the homeless, top medical care for the sick, qualified representation for the incarcerated...

And don't forget – a really big parade!

– James Lloyd

"I remember going through Travis Air Force Base right outside of San Francisco on my way back home and some guy spit on me and screamed that I was a baby killer."

— Marion Stringer, Green Beret

"Let us understand: North Vietnam cannot defeat or humiliate the United States. Only Americans can do that."

— President Richard Nixon

- INVITATION -

Every time you meet Veterans, thank them, all of them. Every time you meet Vietnam Veterans, first apologize, and then thank them.

Laugh
Learn
Live

Torch Tip #37
Live in the now.

"Nothing is more endangered in the modern world than the powerful combination of hard work toward meaningful goals, joined with an exuberant embrace of the present moment."

— Tom Morris

Zen masters use the word *satori* to describe a flash of insight, a moment of total presence. I have been fortunate to have experienced this when I was quiet and alone, surrounded by nature.

The great Zen Master Rinzai asks: "What, at this moment, is lacking?" A similar question in the Zen tradition: "If not now, when?" In *The Power of Now*, Eckhart Tolle delves deeply into this subject.

The Buddhists tell a story of a man running from a ferocious tiger. While the man is fleeing the tiger, he falls off a very steep cliff. Just beyond the edge of the cliff, he grabs onto a single vine. Dangling dangerously, just moments from his death, he looks up and sees a tiger above him. He looks down and sees the jagged rocks, hundreds of feet below. At that very instant he also notices a big, juicy, ripe strawberry growing from the vine he's holding. He grabs the strawberry, begins eating it, and smiles...as he falls.

Wow! That's living in the now!

It seems like people are usually obsessing about their past regrets (creating depression) or constantly worrying about the future (causing anxiety).

Most people spend their lives somewhere other than where they are in the present moment. When we're home, we're thinking about work. When we're at work, we're thinking about the errands we need to run. When we're on vacation, we're thinking about the projects piling up at the office. When we're at the park with our kids, we're thinking about the ball game we're missing on TV.

No wonder we're exhausted!

Try living in the now, and experience the freedom! Living in the present moment holds the key to being free – to be able to live in the now, without guilt or expectation.

Did you ever notice how you can be thinking and thinking, trying to come up with an idea, and then you forget about it for awhile – and later the idea just comes to you? You've got to be still in order to be creative – and by "still," I mean your mind must be clear and peaceful.

Live in the now.

> *"Yesterday is ashes. Tomorrow is wood.*
> *Only today does the fire burn brightly."*
>
> *– an old Eskimo saying*

– I N V I T A T I O N –

Pause your reading and contemplate:
What's going on right here, right now?

Torch Tip #38
Laugh.

Top 5 reasons to laugh:

1) Laughter relaxes us and chases away depression.

> *"Laughter is a tranquilizer with no side effects."*
>
> *– Arnold Glasow*

2) Laughter enhances creativity.

> *"At the height of laughter, the universe is flung into a kaleidoscope of new possibilities."*
>
> *– Jean Houston*

3) Laughter is the ultimate escape.

> *"Laughter is an instant vacation."*
>
> *– Milton Berle*

4) Laughter gives purpose and meaning to life.

> *"The most wasted day is one in which we have not laughed."*
>
> *– Sebastian Chamfort*

5) Laughter is spiritual.

> *"Laughter is the closest thing to the grace of God."*
>
> *– Karl Barth*

*Who among your friends makes you
laugh the most? Thank him.*

Torch Tip #39
Burn candles.

"Life is ours to be spent, not to be saved."

– D.H. Lawrence

You'll be amazed at what candles can do! They create such atmosphere and beauty.

We have a picnic table on our back patio where, on many evenings, Tanya and I relax, play cards, and listen to Pavarotti. We watch the radiant California sun setting in the distance. And you can bet on it – the candles are burning!

I travel a lot, as you may have guessed. Even on the road, some candles and nice music can turn even the most drab hotel room into a glowing retreat center.

You can gaze at a candle and see it as a metaphor for your own "life torch."

A candle is luminous only when it's burning...

...and so are you.

"There isn't enough darkness in all the world
to snuff out the light of one little candle."

– Author unknown

"How far that little candle throws his beams!
So shines a good deed in a weary world."

– William Shakespeare

Got some candles? Burn 'em!

Torch Tip #40
Sleep.

"Take rest. A field that has rested gives a bountiful crop."

— Ovid

How much sleep are you getting? Sleep deprivation is a curse to creativity and a thief to passion.

"Without enough sleep, we all become tall two-year-olds."

— JoJo Jensen

I once belonged to a church where it seemed that the more dedicated one was to Christ, the less he should sleep. Members would boast of their late nights and early mornings. Leaders wore their fatigue like a badge of honor. Come to think of it, we did have our share of tall two-year-olds.

I was one of them.

Take the sleep test. According to Harvard University Economics Professor Juliet Schor, "If you need an alarm clock to wake you in the morning, you're probably sleeping too little."

I get up most mornings without an alarm clock. The solution is simple – earlier to bed! Now of course there's a tradeoff, but it's well worth it. I rarely enjoy Leno's or Letterman's monologue, or catch the late movie, but throughout the next day –

I'm ready to burn!

I've kept this tip brief so you can enjoy a nap.

"The best bridge between despair and hope
is a good night's sleep."

– E. Joseph Cossman

Try going to bed an hour earlier tonight.
Tomorrow, enjoy your energy.

Torch Tip #41
Dance.

*"And when you get the choice to sit it out or dance
I hope you dance, I hope you dance."*

– Leann Womack

I once **BALLROOM** attended a **TAP** conference in
BALLET Southern California **TANGO** called *Come
to the Edge*. There **CLOG** were **LINE** workshops **HULA**
designed **WALTZ** to encourage **POLKA** each of us
SALSA to leave **BELLY** our **SWING** comfort zones.
I **CHARLESTON** checked out **STOMP** the **SLOW**
options and **JIG** chose the **SHIMMY** creative writing
BUNNY HOP experience. As **SHAG** I sat at **MAMBA**
the table **MACARENA** to begin **HIGHLAND FLING**
the class, **CONGA** a friend **BOLERO** strolled up.

"James, why did you choose this workshop? You seem
comfortable and confident as a writer. Instead, which
workshop would you be most nervous to attend?"

"Probably the dancing one. Hmmm."

Five minutes later I strolled reluctantly into a darkened
room, lit only by a few dozen candles. The music was already
playing, and the group was moving in ways I had never
witnessed at high school sock-hops. I stood in terror, too
frightened to join and too resolved to leave. The leader, a
svelte black man about half my age, noticed me and began
to approach. I couldn't believe my eyes! He was wearing a
sheer, black lingerie gown, and his mannerisms were
noticeably effeminate. He invited me to join him. Yikes!

I was raised a conservative Southern Baptist. In an instant, a flood of judgmental taboos were streaming. I had most definitely come to the edge!

And we danced!

And I had a great time!

That day I learned an important lesson. Dancing is not about showing off. It is not about being noticed. It is about having fun expressing your individuality!

"Those who danced were thought to be quite insane by those who could not hear the music."

– Angela Monet

– INVITATION –

You already know this invitation.

Design Your Destiny

Torch Tip #42
Ask yourself: "Why am I here?"

*"There are two great moments in a person's life:
the first is when you are born; the second is when
you discover why you were born."*

– Author unknown

Did you ever notice how close design and destiny are? Your destiny is not just something that happens to you. You are its designer with interior motives.

I remember a time in my life when I was a marketer for a physician recruiting company. I was making more money than ever before, yet something was missing. I was reluctant to change careers because I was over 40 years old, with daughters soon to be in college. For two more years I continued, trying to ignore the nagging of my conscience, "Are you sure this is your calling? Is this what you were born to do?"

When I could no longer ignore my spirit, I chose to pursue my passion. I wanted to be a professional trainer and speaker. That decision included giving up a steady salary and insurance benefits. That first year I made less than half of the prior year. Some of my friends questioned my choice. Even I questioned my choice.

Within two years, all that had changed.

Today, I am living my dream. Both of my daughters are in college. My work is "on purpose." And I no longer hear the haunting cries of a displaced spirit.

"When a man does not know what harbor he is making for, no wind is the right wind."

— Seneca

- I N V I T A T I O N -

Ask yourself, "Why am I here?" Listen...and act.

Torch Tip #43
Choose your age.

*"How old would you be if you didn't know
how old you were?"*

– Satchel Paige

How old are you today, my friend?

Would you like to be younger? You can be!

That's right. You can choose your age. The following quotes contain the clues to avoid the aging process.

*"The great thing about getting older is that
you don't lose all the other ages you've been."*

– Madeleine L'Engle

Because you don't lose all the ages you have been, you can pick which one you desire to be. Your past experience serves as a guide for that age. You remember what you thought, how you felt, the music you loved, etc.

*"You can judge your age by the amount of pain
you feel when you come in contact with a new idea."*

– Pearl Buck

To avoid aging, consider this Pearl Buck quote. How excited are we to consider new ideas? How much pain do we feel when someone presents a new point of view? How open are we to a new concept or paradigm? To remain young, let's strive to keep our minds flexible, even if our bodies are not.

"Those who love deeply never grow old;
they may die of old age, but they die young."

– Sir Arthur Pinero

Here is another clue to choosing our age. The secret lies in our choice to love. Loving deeply is the equivalent of the Fountain of Youth. I have often wondered why the elderly seem to wither and die after they are removed from their families and friends and sent to nursing homes. This quote explains it. Love keeps us young, and loving deeply keeps us even younger.

We all know an 80-year-old youngster, and a 40-year-old senior.

How old do you choose to be?

– INVITATION –

Today, act the age you choose!

Torch Tip #44
Hire a life coach.

"In a sense, coaches are shrinks without the couches, management consultants without the flow charts, and sympathetic bartenders without the row of shot glasses."

– Daniel Pink

Yes, I'm talking about a personal coach...*for your life.* I have an extraordinary coach named Tamara Keefe. It wasn't easy for me to hire her, though. When I first considered it, I kept asking myself...a coach? Just a personal coach? To help...in life? And my friends kept saying, "James, you don't need a coach!"

It's interesting that no one ever said that to me when I was learning to play football or the trumpet. The educational system certainly believes in coaching. Likewise, the corporate world believes that we'll benefit from direction and advice. We have spreadsheets for projects at work – we have handouts and timelines – and a whole team of people to support a project's goals.

But what about the project called "life"?

It's only in this area of our personal lives that people doubt the need for a coach. People are looking for answers and meaning – trying to improve themselves – and they're all attempting this alone! No direction; no support.

When I was debating whether or not to be life-coached, I remember questioning Tamara, "Are you sure you're worth it?" Of course what I was *really* asking was, "Am I worth it?"

Of course I am. And you are worth it, too!

"Your coach will UNLEASH YOU, to become the person you always wanted to be and were capable of becoming."
— *The Coach Connection*

– I N V I T A T I O N –

Contact my life coach, Tamara, for a free 30-minute coaching session. tkeefe12@hotmail.com

Torch Tip #45
Remember your passion.

*"We choose to forget who we are,
and then we forget we've forgotten."*

– Gunther Bernard

There is a horrible disease in the world today. It attacks people of all ages. I have coined it, "Passion Alzheimer's." It's a condition where people can no longer remember their passions or their dreams. They can no longer recall their desires or their purpose.

The fantastic news is that this ailment is curable!

Do you remember your dreams?

Can you recall your passion?

If you need a refresher course, read the book *Discover Your Passion* by Gail Cassidy.

And scan over again some of the tips in this book. There's a lot of passion glowing on these pages.

Find the spark that will rekindle your passion. Rejuvenate yourself.

In one of his last interviews, the truly inspirational Christopher Reeve talked about the frustration he felt when he saw an able-bodied person who was paralyzed in other ways. He said that he wanted to tell that person to just *get up and go for it!*

Remember your passion.

*"Cherish your visions and your dreams
as they are the children of your Soul..."*

– Napoleon Hill

– I N V I T A T I O N –

What did you dream about as a child?

Epilogue

So, how do you view your life now?

Is it a candle...or is it a torch?

Has the flicker grown into a flame?

Is the fire burning more brightly?

I'd like to end where we began, with our magnificent Shaw quote:

*"I am of the opinion that my life belongs to the whole community...
as long as I live, it is my privilege to do for it whatever I can. I
want to be thoroughly used up when I die. For the harder I work,
the more I live. I rejoice in life, for its own sake. Life is no brief
candle to me; it is a splendid torch, which I've got hold of for the
moment. And I want to make it burn as brightly as possible,
before handing it on to future generations."*

My hope is that you have been encouraged to burn your torch just a little brighter.

Thank you so much for reading, for having an open mind, and for desiring to live life to its fullest.

And thank you for allowing me this opportunity to share my torch tips – and my life – with you, my fellow torch-bearers.

I am honored.

Finally...

If someone gave this book to you, you are loved.
If I gave this book to you, you are loved.
If you gave this book to yourself, you are loved.

Keep burning brightly,

www.9screens.com

Extra Fuel

*"The real measure of your wealth is how much
you'd be worth if you lost all your money."*

— *Bernard Meltzer*

*"The only way of discovering the limits of the possible is to
venture a little way past them into the impossible."*

— *Arthur C. Clarke*

*"A childlike man is not a man whose development
has been arrested; on the contrary, he is a man who
has given himself a chance of continuing to develop
long after most adults have muffled themselves
in the cocoon of middle-aged habit and convention."*

— *Aldous Huxley*

*"He is a man of sense who does not grieve for what he has not,
but rejoices in what he has."*

— *Epictetus*

"Become the change you wish to see in others."

— *Mahatma Gandhi*

"Nothing happens unless first a dream."

– Carl Sandburg

"There are two days that no one should ever worry about:
yesterday and tomorrow."

– Robert Burdette

"Angels sail through our lives like ships of light,
visiting us through portals of our heart."

– Karen Goldman

"There are many ways to measure success; not the least of which is
the way your child describes you when talking to a friend."

– Author unknown

"Every man's work, whether it be literature or music or pictures
or architecture or anything else, is always a portrait of himself."

– Samuel Butler

"Much may be known of a man's character
by what excites his laughter."

– Goethe

"The mediocre teacher tells. The good teacher explains. The superior teacher demonstrates. The great teacher inspires."

— William A. Ward

"Some people say they haven't yet found themselves. But the self is not something one finds; it is something one creates."

— Thomas Szasz

"Our lives begin to end the day we become silent about things that matter."

— Dr. Martin Luther King, Jr.

"I would rather be ashes than dust! I would rather that my spark should burn out in a brilliant blaze than it should be stifled by dry-rot. I would rather be a superb meteor, every atom of me in magnificent glow, than a sleepy and permanent planet. The proper function of man is to live, not to exist. I shall not waste my days in trying to prolong them. I shall use my time."

— Jack London

"Of all earthly music, that which reaches farthest into heaven is the beating of a truly loving heart."

— Henry Ward Beecher

*"What this power is, I cannot say. All I know is that it exists...
and it becomes available only when you are in that state of mind
in which you know EXACTLY what you want...and are fully
determined not to quit until you get it."*

— Alexander Graham Bell

*"Life is a great big canvas, and you should throw
all the paint you can on it."*

— Danny Kaye

*"Twenty years from now you will be more disappointed
by the things that you didn't do than by the ones you did do.
So throw off the bowlines. Sail away from the safe harbor.
Catch the trade winds in your sails.
Explore. Dream. Discover."*

— Mark Twain

"The only way to know the future is to invent it yourself."

— Barbara Roberts

*"I will make love my greatest weapon and none on who I call
can defend against its force....My love will melt all hearts liken
to the sun whose rays soften the coldest day."*

— Og Mandino

"*The intuitive mind is a sacred gift and the rational mind is a faithful servant. We have created a society that honors the servant and has forgotten the gift.*"

– Albert Einstein

"*Seek out that particular mental attribute which makes you feel most deeply and vitally alive, along with which comes the inner voice which says, 'This is the real me,' and when you have found that attitude, follow it.*"

– William James

"*Love one another, and you'll be happy. It's as simple – and as difficult – as that.*"

– Michael Leunig

"*This nation was built by men who took risks; pioneers who were not afraid of the wilderness, business men who were not afraid of failure, scientists who were not afraid of the truth, thinkers who were not afraid of progress, dreamers who were not afraid of action.*"

– Brooks Atkinson

"*None are so old as those who have outlived enthusiasm.*"

– Henry David Thoreau

– SPECIAL INVITATION –

I encourage you to visit me online at

www.9screens.com

where you'll find:

- MY BOOKS

- MY CDs

- KEYNOTE SPEECHES

- TRAINING SESSIONS

- FREE GIFTS

- PLUS MUCH MORE

Enter code "TT" for a 20% discount!!!

Thanks again for allowing me the opportunity to serve you.